GRADE
5

240 Vocabulary Words
Kids Need to Know

24 Ready-to-Reproduce Packets
That Make
Vocabulary Building
Fun & Effective

by Linda Ward Beech

■SCHOLASTIC
Teaching
Resources

New York • Toronto • London • Auckland • Sydney
Mexico City • New Delhi • Hong Kong • Buenos Aires

Cover design by Gerard Fuchs

Interior design by Melinda Belter

Interior illustrations by Steve Cox, Mike Moran

ISBN: 0-439-28045-I

15 16 17 18 19 20 21 22 23 24   40   12 11

GRADE 5 | Table of Contents

Using the Book

Where would we be without words? It's hard to imagine. Words are a basic building block of communication, and a strong vocabulary is an essential part of reading, writing, and speaking well. The purpose of this book is to help learners expand the number of words they know and the ways in which they use them. Although 240 vocabulary words are introduced, many more words and meanings are woven into the book's 24 lessons.

Learning new words is not just about encountering them; it's about using them, exploring them, and thinking about them. So the lessons in this book are organized around different aspects and attributes of words—related meanings, how words are formed, where words come from, acronyms, homophones, homographs, word parts, clips, blends, and much more. The lessons provide an opportunity for students to try out words, reflect on words, and have fun with words.

Materials: As you introduce the lessons, be sure to have the following items available:

> **dictionaries**
> **thesauruses**
> **writing notebooks or journals**
> **writing tools**

TIP You'll find a complete alphabetized list of all the lesson words at the back of the book.

Lesson Organization: Each lesson is three pages long and introduces ten words.

The first lesson page includes:

lesson words

statement of lesson focus

simple sentences explaining the meanings of the words

two exercises

The second page includes:

lesson words

cloze activity

thinking activity with test prep fill-ins

Writing to Learn component

The third page includes:

puzzle, game, or other learning activity using the words

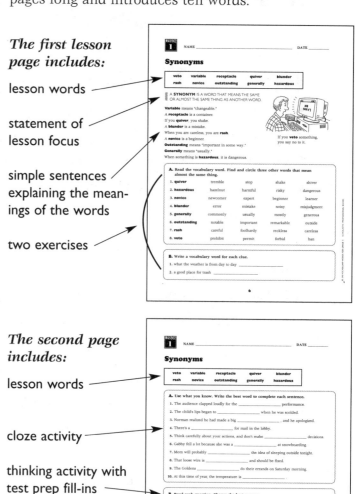

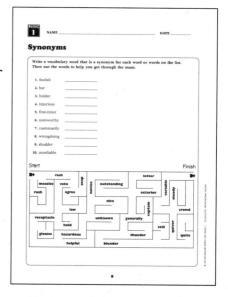

Tips for Using the Lessons:

- Many words have more than one meaning, including some that are not given in the lesson. You may want to point out additional meanings or invite students to discover them independently.

- Many words can be used as more than one part of speech. Again, you can expand students' vocabulary by drawing attention to such usage.

- As you go over the exercises with students, discuss all the choices that are given and why some of them are the wrong answers. In some cases, students may have to look up words in order to determine if a choice is correct or not.

- Have students complete the Writing to Learn activities in a notebook or journal so they have a specific place where they can refer to and review words.

- Consider having students make a set of word cards for each lesson, or make a class set and place it in your writing center.

- Build word family lists with words based on major phonograms such as *fan, champ,* or *mike.*

- Don't hesitate to add your own writing assignments. The more students use a word, the more likely they are to "own" it.

- Be aware of pronunciation differences when teaching homographs. Not all students may pronounce words in the same way and this can lead to confusion.

- Use the words to teach syllabication rules.

- Use the words to teach related spelling and grammar rules.

- Encourage students to make semantic maps for some words. For instance, students might organize a map for a noun to show what the word is, what it is like, what it is not like, and include some examples of the word.

- Have students illustrate some words.

- Help students make connections by pointing out lesson words used in other contexts and materials.

- Talk about other forms of a word, for example *optimum, optimistic, optimist, optimally.* Encourage students to word build in this fashion.

- Have students locate places on a world map when studying words from other languages.

- Have students categorize words.

- Encourage students to consult more than one reference and to compare information.

TIP Consider having students fill out Word Inventory Sheets before each lesson. The headings for such a sheet might be: Words I Know; Words I Have Seen but Don't Really Know; New Words. Using pencils, students can list the vocabulary words and probable meanings under the headings. As the lesson proceeds, they can make revisions and additions.

Synonyms

veto	variable	receptacle	quiver	blunder
rash	novice	outstanding	generally	hazardous

█ A **SYNONYM** IS A WORD THAT MEANS THE SAME
OR ALMOST THE SAME THING AS ANOTHER WORD.

Variable means "changeable."

A **receptacle** is a container.

If you **quiver**, you shake.

A **blunder** is a mistake.

When you are careless, you are **rash**.

A **novice** is a beginner.

Outstanding means "important in some way."

Generally means "usually."

When something is **hazardous**, it is dangerous.

If you **veto** something,
you say no to it.

A. Read the vocabulary word. Find and circle three other words that mean almost the same thing.

1. **quiver**	tremble	stop	shake	shiver
2. **hazardous**	hazelnut	harmful	risky	dangerous
3. **novice**	newcomer	expert	beginner	learner
4. **blunder**	error	mistake	noisy	misjudgment
5. **generally**	commonly	usually	mostly	generous
6. **outstanding**	notable	important	remarkable	outside
7. **rash**	careful	foolhardy	reckless	careless
8. **veto**	prohibit	permit	forbid	ban

B. Write a vocabulary word for each clue.

1. what the weather is from day to day _____

2. a good place for trash _____

Synonyms

veto	variable	receptacle	quiver	blunder
rash	novice	outstanding	generally	hazardous

A. Use what you know. Write the best word to complete each sentence.

1. The audience clapped loudly for the _____ performance.

2. The child's lips began to _____ when he was scolded.

3. Norman realized he had made a big _____ , and he apologized.

4. There's a _____ for mail in the lobby.

5. Think carefully about your actions, and don't make _____ decisions.

6. Gabby fell a lot because she was a _____ at snowboarding.

7. Mom will probably _____ the idea of sleeping outside tonight.

8. That loose wire is _____ and should be fixed.

9. The Goldens _____ do their errands on Saturday morning.

10. At this time of year, the temperature is _____ .

B. Read each question. Choose the best answer.

1. Which one is a novice?   ❏ pro   ❏ old-timer   ❏ rookie

2. Which one is hazardous?   ❏ poison   ❏ portrait   ❏ porridge

3. What makes you quiver?   ❏ food   ❏ fear   ❏ fun

4. Which one is a receptacle?   ❏ rug   ❏ rag   ❏ bag

✏ Writing to Learn

Design and write a warning sign. Use at least two vocabulary words.

NAME _____ DATE _____

Synonyms

Write a vocabulary word that is a synonym for each word or words on the list. Then use the words to help you get through the maze.

1. foolish _____

2. bar _____

3. holder _____

4. injurious _____

5. first-timer _____

6. noteworthy _____

7. customarily _____

8. wrongdoing _____

9. shudder _____

10. unreliable _____

Start   Finish

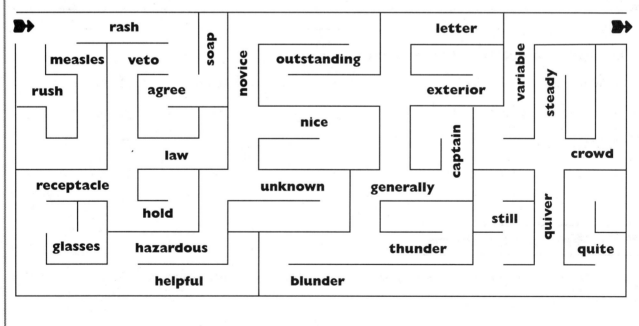

Synonyms

| brutal | daunting | treacherous | bewildered | bountiful |
| blissful | valid | cumbersome | dormant | ceaseless |

▌A **SYNONYM** IS A WORD THAT MEANS THE SAME
OR ALMOST THE SAME AS ANOTHER WORD.

Brutal means "cruel."

When someone is **treacherous**, that person is false.

When you are **bewildered**, you're confused.

Bountiful means "plentiful."

If you are happy, you are **blissful**.

Something that is **valid** is true.

Cumbersome means "clumsy."

Dormant means "sleeping."

Something that is **ceaseless** is unending.

If a task is **daunting**,
it is discouraging.

A. Read the words in each row. Write a
vocabulary word that means almost the
same thing.

1. continuing, perpetual _____

2. puzzled, perplexed _____

3. deceptive, traitorous _____

4. wonderful, delightful _____

5. dismaying, disheartening _____

6. plentiful, ample _____

7. proven, confirmed _____

8. inhuman, pitiless _____

B. Write a vocabulary word
that describes each picture.

1.

_____

2.

_____

Synonyms

brutal	daunting	treacherous	bewildered	bountiful
blissful	valid	cumbersome	dormant	ceaseless

A. Use what you know. Write the best word to complete each sentence.

1. The large suitcase was awkward and _____ to carry.

2. During rush hour, the traffic went on and on; it was _____ .

3. Cricket offered a sound and _____ argument for her case.

4. This year, the harvest was rich and _____ .

5. Crossing the rope bridge presented a _____ challenge to Marv.

6. By telling secrets about others, Sam turned out to be a _____ friend.

7. The treatment of prisoners in some places is _____ .

8. Sitting by the fire after a good meal made the skiers feel _____ .

9. The driver was _____ by all the signs at the intersection.

10. During the winter, many plants are _____ .

B. Read each question. Choose the best answer.

1. Which one is blissful? ❏ bridge ❏ bride ❏ bribe

2. Which one is ceaseless? ❏ waterfall ❏ watchword ❏ water drop

3. Which one is bewildered? ❏ expert ❏ teacher ❏ beginner

4. Which one is bountiful? ❏ famine ❏ feast ❏ failure

✎ Writing to Learn

Write a comic strip about a detective. Use at least three vocabulary words.

Synonyms

Play a game of Move On. Find a word in the first box that does not have the same meaning as the other three words. Move that word to the next box by writing it on the blank line. The first one is done for you. Continue until you reach the last box. Complete the sentence in that box.

Start here.

bewildered blissful confused muddled	_____blissful_____ joyous dormant delighted	suspended treacherous sleeping _____
There are many _____ reasons for having a good vocabulary.		_____ disloyal bountiful unfaithful
clumsy _____ valid burdensome		generous _____ abundant brutal
endless cumbersome incessant _____	_____ terrifying discouraging ceaseless	cruel savage _____ daunting

Antonyms

criticism	unique	flimsy	allow	fatigue
compliment	ordinary	substantial	prohibit	vigor

▌ AN **ANTONYM** IS A WORD THAT MEANS
THE OPPOSITE OF ANOTHER WORD.

You give a **compliment** when you say something good, but offer
criticism when you make an unfavorable remark.

If something is **unique**, it is the only one, but something
ordinary is common.

If something is **flimsy**, it is frail, but if it is **substantial**, it is solid.

Allow is the opposite of **prohibit**.

Fatigue is weariness, and **vigor** is strength.

Prohibit means "forbid."

A. Read each word. Write a word
from the box that is an antonym.

unmatched	prevent	firm	permit
praise	energy	weak	disapproval

1. **flimsy**   _____

2. **ordinary**   _____

3. **prohibit**   _____

4. **compliment** _____

5. **allow**   _____

6. **fatigue**   _____

7. **criticism**   _____

8. **substantial** _____

B. Read the words in each box below.
Underline the two words in each
box that are antonyms.

1. | exhaustion | vigor | vitamin |

2. | union | usual | unique |

3. | allow | give | forbid |

4. | enemy | flimsy | sturdy |

NAME _____ DATE _____

Antonyms

criticism	unique	flimsy	allow	fatigue
compliment	ordinary	substantial	prohibit	vigor

A. Use what you know. Write the best word to complete each sentence.

1. Wendy gave Jack a _____ when his project won a prize.

2. The neighbors don't _____ us to play ball on their lawn.

3. Don is always full of vim and _____ .

4. Although it was an _____ glass, Mom was sorry about breaking it.

5. After a hard workout, Noah felt a sense of _____ .

6. The owner is happy because her shop made a _____ profit this year.

7. Those signs _____ cars from driving in the park at certain hours.

8. The piano student knew she would receive _____ because she hadn't practiced.

9. Each piece of pottery is _____ because it is made by hand.

10. Everyone was annoyed when the girls gave only a _____ excuse for being late.

B. Read each question. Choose the best answer.

1. Which one is the most substantial? ☐ tent ☐ house ☐ hut

2. Which one is pleasing? ☐ complaint ☐ criticism ☐ compliment

3. What causes fatigue? ☐ jumping ☐ sleeping ☐ resting

4. Which painting is unique? ☐ copy ☐ original ☐ reproduction

 Writing to Learn

Write two cause-and-effect statements. Use two vocabulary words in each.

Antonyms

Rewrite Joy's e-mail to her cousin. Use an antonym for each underlined word.

Hey Seth,

Thanks for your <u>criticism</u> about my decision to take juggling lessons instead of going out for soccer again. Everyone plays soccer—I want to be <u>ordinary</u>. And even though I practice a lot, I never feel the <u>vigor</u> that comes from an afternoon on the soccer field.

My biggest problem is getting Mom to <u>prohibit</u> me to juggle indoors. For some reason, she thinks I will break stuff! :-) I am beginning with small balls but hope to juggle <u>flimsy</u> things by the time I see you.

Joy

_____

_____

_____

_____

_____

_____

_____

Antonyms

frisky	permanent	tiresome	considerate	ridiculous
sluggish	unstable	interesting	heedless	sensible

▌ AN **ANTONYM** IS A WORD THAT MEANS
THE OPPOSITE OF ANOTHER WORD.

Frisky means "lively," but **sluggish** means "slow."

Permanent means "lasting."

If something is **tiresome**, it's boring; if it holds
your attention, it's **interesting**.

Someone who is **considerate** is thoughtful, but
someone who is **heedless** is not.

If you're **sensible**, you're wise, and if you're silly,
you're **ridiculous**.

It means "tipsy!"

Unstable means "unsteady."

A. Read the word in the first column. Find and circle the word in the row that
is an antonym.

1. **frisky**	frittering	freezing	inactive
2. **unstable**	unable	precarious	settled
3. **ridiculous**	wise	laughable	rickety
4. **interesting**	boring	inviting	intense
5. **sensible**	logical	separate	ridiculous
6. **considerate**	careful	continuing	thoughtless

B. Read the word in the first column. Circle the word that is an antonym,
and underline the word that is a synonym.

1. **permanent**	a. unsettled	b. stable	c. perfect
2. **sluggish**	a. hit	b. lazy	c. playful
3. **heedless**	a. thoughtful	b. headless	c. inconsiderate
4. **tiresome**	a. dull	b. talkative	c. fascinating

Antonyms

frisky	permanent	tiresome	considerate	ridiculous
sluggish	unstable	interesting	heedless	sensible

A. Use what you know. Write the best word to complete each sentence.

1. It was kind and _____ of Judd to give his seat to me.

2. The _____ puppy ran around and jumped on everyone.

3. Don't skate on the pond because the ice becomes _____ as it melts.

4. Sasha felt _____ when she noticed she had on two different socks.

5. The hot, humid weather made everyone feel idle and _____ .

6. Clark found the speaker very _____ because he kept repeating himself.

7. After traveling so much, Mr. Page was glad to have a _____ home.

8. The child ran down the sidewalk, _____ of his mother's calls.

9. If the forecast is for rain, be _____ and take your umbrella.

10. You need a good beginning to make your report more _____ .

B. Read each question. Choose the best answer.

1. What is a kitten like?   ❑ sensible   ❑ frisky   ❑ considerate

2. Which one is permanent?   ❑ ink   ❑ pencil   ❑ chalk

3. What's a hibernating bear like? ❑ sloppy   ❑ active   ❑ sluggish

4. What makes a beach unstable?   ❑ waves   ❑ shells   ❑ gulls

✍ Writing to Learn

Write a want ad for a lost pet. Use at least three vocabulary words.

Antonyms

Play Tic-Tac-Antonym. Read each word. Then draw a line through three words in the box that are antonyms for that word. Your line can be vertical, horizontal, or diagonal.

1. frisky

busy	nosy	playful
slow	sluggish	idle
happy	frilly	frizzy

2. sensible

rowdy	smart	absurd
serious	neat	rash
sensitive	sorry	ridiculous

3. permanent

perfect	fearful	interrupted
lasting	unstable	curly
impermanent	forever	perfume

4. interesting

intentional	delightful	exceptional
exciting	curious	investing
dull	tiresome	uninteresting

5. considerate

inattentive	careless	heedless
impressed	fragile	casual
gifted	hopeful	concerned

Compound Words

earthquake	vineyard	whirlpool	headquarters	guidebook
touchdown	blueprint	spellbound	masterpiece	windshield

▌ A **COMPOUND WORD** IS A WORD MADE UP
OF TWO SMALLER WORDS PUT TOGETHER.

An **earthquake** is a shaking of the ground caused by
a movement of the plates beneath Earth's surface.

A **vineyard** is a field where grapes are grown.

A **whirlpool** is a current of water that spins around rapidly.

A **headquarters** is a command post for a group.

A **guidebook** is a book of information for tourists.

A **blueprint** is a plan for a building.

Spellbound means "enchanted."

A **masterpiece** is something made with great skill.

The front window of a car is called a **windshield**.

A **touchdown** is a score in
a football game.

A. Complete each sentence with a vocabulary word.

1. A shield from the wind is a _____.

2. A book that's a guide is a _____.

3. A quake of the earth is an _____.

4. A print that is blue is a _____.

5. A yard where vines grow is a _____.

6. A pool that whirls around is a _____.

7. A piece by a master is a _____.

B. Write the two words that make up each compound word.

1. **headquarters**   2. **touchdown**   3. **spellbound**

_____   _____   _____

_____   _____   _____

© 240 VOCABULARY WORDS FOR GRADE 5   SCHOLASTIC PROFESSIONAL BOOKS

Compound Words

earthquake	vineyard	whirlpool	headquarters	guidebook
touchdown	blueprint	spellbound	masterpiece	windshield

A. Use what you know. Write the best word to complete each sentence.

1. Please report to _____ before beginning your work.

2. The visitors opened their _____ to read about the city.

3. Mrs. Drew peered through the _____ to see the road.

4. The home team scored a _____ to win the game.

5. Roger planted a _____ behind the farmhouse.

6. Although the _____ was brief, it shook the house.

7. The artist considers this painting to be her _____ .

8. The children watched _____ as the magician performed.

9. The architect prepared a _____ of the proposed concert hall.

10. A leaf caught in the _____ spun around and disappeared.

B. Read each question. Choose the best answer.

1. Which one protects you? ❑ windmill ❑ windstorm ❑ windshield

2. Which one is a drawing? ❑ blueprint ❑ bluefish ❑ blueberry

3. Which one makes a touchdown? ❑ headquarters ❑ quarterback ❑ quartermaster

4. What's in a vineyard? ❑ animals ❑ vegetables ❑ fruit

✐ Writing to Learn

Write a guidebook entry about a real or imaginary place. Use at least two vocabulary words.

Compound Words

Write the vocabulary word for each clue. Then write the circled letters on the numbered lines at the bottom of the page to answer the riddle.

WHAT GOES UP AND DOWN BUT DOESN'T MOVE?

1. a natural disaster ___ ___ ___ ___ ___ ___ ___ ___ ___

2. found above a car hood ___ ___ ___ ___ ___ ___ ___ ___

3. a great work of art ___ ___ ___ ___ ___ ___ ___ ___ ___

4. a kind of farm ___ ___ ___ ___ ___ ___ ___

5. dangerous water ___ ___ ___ ___ ___ ___ ___ ___

6. a diagram of a place ___ ___ ___ ___ ___ ___ ___ ___

7. between the goalposts ___ ___ ___ ___ ___ ___ ___ ___

8. a kind of office ___ ___ ___ ___ ___ ___ ___ ___ ___ ___

9. fascinated ___ ___ ___ ___ ___ ___ ___ ___

10. a handy book for travelers ___ ___ ___ ___ ___ ___ ___ ___

___ ___ ___ ___ ___ ___ ___ ___ ___ ___
 1   2   3   4   5   6   7   8   9   10

Homophones

lute	cruise	foul	course	bridal
loot	crews	fowl	coarse	bridle

▌A **HOMOPHONE** IS A WORD THAT SOUNDS LIKE ANOTHER WORD BUT HAS A DIFFERENT MEANING, SPELLING, AND ORIGIN.

A **lute** is a musical instrument.

Loot means "to rob or steal."

A **cruise** is a trip on a ship.

Groups of people working together are **crews**.

Something that is **foul** is unclean.

A **course** is a direction or movement.

Coarse is the opposite of fine.

Bridal means "related to a wedding."

A **bridle** is used to control a horse.

A **fowl** is a bird such as a goose.

A. Complete each riddle with a vocabulary word. Use the pictures to help you.

1. I sound like *bridal,* but I am a

   _____ .

2. I sound like *loot,* but I am a

   _____ .

3. I sound like *fowl,* but I am a

   _____ .

4. I sound like *crews,* but I am used for a

   _____ .

B. Write a vocabulary word for each clue.

1. I am a path you might take. _____

2. I describe something rough. _____

NAME _____   DATE _____

Homophones

lute	cruise	foul	course	bridal
loot	crews	fowl	coarse	bridle

A. Use what you know. Write the best vocabulary word to complete each sentence.

1. Work _____ were sent out to repair potholes in the streets.

2. The smelly junkyard was a _____ place.

3. My sister's _____ gown is very beautiful.

4. The Rosens are going on a _____ to celebrate their anniversary.

5. The builders use _____ sand to make cement.

6. In this painting of long ago, a girl is playing the _____ .

7. Chickens are the main _____ raised on this farm.

8. Barry slipped the _____ over his horse's head.

9. The burglars were foiled in their plot to _____ a jewelry store.

10. This river follows a winding _____ to the sea.

B. Read each question. Choose the best answer.

1. Which one quacks?   ❏ foul   ❏ fowl   ❏ foal

2. Who's in a bridal party?   ❏ graduate   ❏ grocer   ❏ groom

3. Which one has strings?   ❏ flute   ❏ lute   ❏ loot

4. Who works in crews?   ❏ rowers   ❏ rulers   ❏ readers

Writing to Learn

Find another meaning for at least three vocabulary words. Use the words with their new meanings in sentences.

NAME _____ DATE _____

Homophones

These book titles have errors in them. Rewrite each title so it is correct.

1.

A Bridal for My Horse

_____
_____
_____

2.

How to Play the Loot

_____
_____
_____

3.

Planning a Coarse for a Vacation Crews

_____
_____
_____

4.

Fowl Play!
The Story of Cruise That Lute Bridle Parties

_____
_____
_____

5.

Tips for Raising Foul

_____
_____
_____

6.

Using Burlap and Other Course Fabrics

_____
_____
_____

NAME _____ DATE _____

Homographs

present	minute	refuse	invalid	object
present	minute	refuse	invalid	object

A **HOMOGRAPH** IS A WORD THAT IS SPELLED THE SAME AS ANOTHER WORD BUT HAS A DIFFERENT MEANING AND SOMETIMES A DIFFERENT PRONUNCIATION.

If you **present** something, you give it.

When you are **present,** you are there in person.

Refuse is garbage.

If you **refuse** to do something, you won't do it.

An **invalid** is someone who is sick.

Something is **invalid** when it is no longer in force.

If you **object** to something, you oppose it.

An **object** is something you can see or touch.

Something that is **minute** is very small.

A **minute** is a measure of time.

A. Read each sentence. Then circle the correct word.

1. The invalid was too ill to get out of bed.   **a.** in′ və ləd   **b.** in va′ləd

2. Mom does not object to driving us to the movies.   **a.** äb′ jikt   **b.** əb jekt′

3. Every minute counts in a race.   **a.** mī nüt′   **b.** mi′ nət

4. Hannah wants to present flowers to the teacher.   **a.** pre′ zənt   **b.** pri zent′

5. The twins refuse to wear the same clothes.   **a.** ri fyüz′   **b.** re′ fyüs

6. How many class members are present today?   **a.** pre′ zənt   **b.** pri zent′

B. Write a vocabulary word for each underlined word.

1. This old passport is <u>worthless</u>.   _____

2. The man was carrying a large <u>item.</u>   _____

3. Put your <u>trash</u> in the container.   _____

4. The dollhouse had <u>tiny</u> dishes.   _____

NAME _____ DATE _____

Homographs

present	minute	refuse	invalid	object
present	minute	refuse	invalid	object

A. Use what you know. Write the best word to complete each sentence.

1. You must sign a check, or it will be _____ .

2. The principal will _____ awards at the assembly.

3. An ambulance took the _____ to the hospital.

4. Sylvia will be here in just one _____ .

5. What is that large _____ in the middle of the road?

6. If you are full, you can _____ a second helping.

7. The spot is so _____ , you can hardly see it.

8. Here comes the sanitation truck to pick up the _____ .

9. Loretta wasn't _____ when we got the assignment.

10. Dad will _____ if you come to dinner with dirty hands.

B. Read each question. Choose the best answer.

1. Is an invalid invalid?   ❑ yes   ❑ no

2. If you're present, can you present?   ❑ yes   ❑ no

3. Can an object object?   ❑ yes   ❑ no

4. Can refuse refuse something?   ❑ yes   ❑ no

 Writing to Learn

Explain why homographs can be confusing. Give some tips for understanding them. Use at least three homographs as examples.

Homographs

Are you a homograph hound? Read each sentence. Circle the number beside the correct meaning for each underlined word. If the numbers you circle add up to 15, you're a winner and a homograph hound!

My score: _____

1. Please plan to be <u>present</u> at the meeting tomorrow.

   1. make an appearance   **2.** give a gift

2. Peg <u>refuses</u> to sing in public because she is shy.

   1. rubbish   **2.** declines

3. Kareem was glad to recover because he didn't like being an <u>invalid</u>.

   1. sick person   **2.** null and void

4. It's a surprise party so don't be a <u>minute</u> late.

   1. something tiny   **2.** one-sixtieth of an hour

5. This document is outdated and <u>invalid</u>.

   1. in poor health   **2.** not in effect

6. Mom <u>objects</u> to letting the dog in the living room.

   1. is against   **2.** a thing

7. Even though it was a <u>minute</u> scratch, the child still cried.

   1. really small   **2.** 60 seconds

8. Kathy will <u>present</u> the trophy to the winner.

   1. appear   **2.** deliver

9. The <u>refuse</u> is collected from the curb on Mondays and Thursdays.

   1. waste material   **2.** reject

10. On the shelf were some vases and other <u>objects</u>.

    1. opposition   **2.** articles

© 240 VOCABULARY WORDS FOR GRADE 5   SCHOLASTIC PROFESSIONAL BOOKS

Eponyms

sardines	tuxedo	vaudeville	bikini	marathon
cologne	bologna	tarantula	tangerine	cantaloupe

▌ AN **EPONYM** IS A WORD THAT COMES FROM
THE NAME OF A PERSON OR PLACE.

Sardines are small fish often packed in cans for sale.

Vaudeville is a variety show.

A **bikini** is a small, two-piece bathing suit.

A **marathon** is a running race of just over 26 miles.

Cologne is a fragrant liquid. / **Bologna** is a lunch meat.

A **tarantula** is a large hairy spider with a poisonous bite.

A **tangerine** is an orange-colored citrus fruit. / A **cantaloupe** is a melon.

A **tuxedo** is a
kind of dress coat.

A. Write a vocabulary word for each sentence.

1. Delicious melons were first grown on an estate named
   Cantalopo in Italy.   _____

2. A runner raced 26 miles to Athens with news of victory
   at the Battle of Marathon in ancient Greece.   _____

3. A composer gained fame for his songs at Vau-de-Vire in France. _____

4. Men in Tuxedo, New York, wore a new style of dinner jacket
   in the late 1800s.   _____

5. A light fragrance was made in Cologne, Germany.   _____

6. A small saltwater fish was found near the island of Sardinia. _____

B. Draw a line to match each word with its name story.

1. **bikini**   a. A sweet fruit was first found in Tangiers in Africa.

2. **tarantula**   b. Bologna, a city in Italy, is where a lightly smoked meat
                          sausage was made.

3. **bologna**   c. People on the island of Bikini in the Pacific Ocean wear few
                          clothes because of the warm climate.

4. **tangerine**   d. Taranto, Italy, is known for its spiders.

Eponyms

sardines	tuxedo	vaudeville	bikini	marathon
cologne	bologna	tarantula	tangerine	cantaloupe

A. Use what you know. Write the best word to complete each sentence.

1. Jenny dabbed some _____ behind her ears before the party.

2. Hector worked out daily in preparation for the _____ .

3. Do they serve _____ sandwiches in the cafeteria?

4. Like other spiders, a _____ has eight legs and no wings.

5. Mr. Ricci grows several kinds of melons, including _____ .

6. Mom asked us to buy a can of _____ at the store.

7. The entertainers put on a real _____ show.

8. For his prom, my brother is renting a _____ .

9. Sonia tried on a _____ in the swim shop.

10. I packed a _____ in my knapsack to peel and eat on the hike.

B. Read each question. Choose the best answer.

1. Which one is formal?   ❐ sweater   ❐ tuxedo   ❐ bikini

2. Which one is tiring?   ❐ marinate   ❐ maritime   ❐ marathon

3. Which one is dangerous?   ❐ tangerine   ❐ tarantella   ❐ tarantula

4. Which one has fins?   ❐ sapphire   ❐ sardine   ❐ sarcasm

👓 Writing to Learn

Find out more about the history of one of the vocabulary words and the place for which it is named. Write a paragraph to report on your research.

© 240 VOCABULARY WORDS FOR GRADE 5   SCHOLASTIC PROFESSIONAL BOOKS

LESSON 8

NAME _____ DATE _____

Eponyms

Read each list of words. Write a vocabulary word to go with each group.

1. _____

towel

lotion

umbrella

2. _____

hairy

legs

eggs

3. _____

lemon

grapefruit

orange

4. _____

perfume

lipstick

rouge

5. _____

prom

wedding

ball

6. _____

ocean

net

food

7. _____

ham

salami

pastrami

8. _____

concert

play

opera

9. _____

distance

challenge

race

10. _____

honeydew

rind

watermelon

© 240 VOCABULARY WORDS FOR GRADE 5   SCHOLASTIC PROFESSIONAL BOOKS

29

Words From Other Cultures

alligator	bandit	syrup	pajamas	okra
barbecue	magazine	sheik	kimono	impala

MANY WORDS IN ENGLISH COME FROM THE
LANGUAGES OF **OTHER CULTURES.**

Words From Spanish An **alligator** is a large reptile with
leathery skin.

A **barbecue** is an outdoor grill
for cooking meat.

Words From Arabic A **magazine** is a publication for reading.

Syrup is a sweet thick liquid such as molasses.

A **sheik** is the chief or head of a family.

Word From Persian **Pajamas** are clothes worn for sleeping.

Word From Japanese A **kimono** is a long outer garment worn in Japan.

Words From Africa **Okra** is a plant used in stew or soup.

Impala is a word from the Zulu people of Africa.

A **bandit** is a robber.
(From Arabic)

A. Write *Arabic, Japanese, African,* or
Persian to tell where the word for
each picture is from.

1.
_____

2.
_____

3.
_____

4.
_____

5.
_____

6.
_____

B. Write a vocabulary word to
complete each sentence.

1. The Arabic word *makhazin* means
"storehouse." A _____ is a
storehouse of articles.

2. In Spanish, *el lagarto* means "lizard." An
_____ looks like a lizard.

3. The Arabic word *shaykh* originally
meant "old man." A leader such as a
_____ is usually an older man.

4. The Spanish word *barbacoa* means a
"frame of sticks." The first outdoor
_____ were over open fires
made of sticks.

Words From Other Cultures

alligator	bandit	syrup	pajamas	okra
barbecue	magazine	sheik	kimono	impala

A. Use what you know. Write the best word to complete each sentence.

1. We saw a log in the river that turned out to be a real _____ .

2. Macy poured _____ on her pancakes.

3. Tony subscribes to a _____ about sports.

4. Dad plans to _____ steaks on the Fourth of July.

5. The children were in their _____ when Greta arrived to baby-sit.

6. A masked _____ was the villain in that movie.

7. Mrs. Say wore a beautiful silk _____ that she bought in Japan.

8. The picture shows an _____ running across the African plains.

9. Mrs. Watkins served _____ as a vegetable with supper.

10. The _____ spoke to his people about a problem in the village.

B. Read each question. Choose the best answer.

1. Which one's for nighttime?   ❑ paisley   ❑ pajamas   ❑ kimono

2. Which one adds taste?   ❑ symbol   ❑ synonym   ❑ syrup

3. Which one's informative?   ❑ magnolia   ❑ magnet   ❑ magazine

4. Which one's from Africa?   ❑ eagle   ❑ impala   ❑ horse

Writing to Learn

Pretend you are planning a display window for a store or museum. Write a description of what the display topic is and what you will include. Use at least two vocabulary words.

Words From Other Cultures

Read the clues. Write the word next to the clue. Then find and circle each word in the puzzle.

```
B  D  J  T  M  Q  A  V  C  M  X  P  S
A  L  L  I  G  A  T  O  R  L  O  W  Y
R  F  R  E  K  W  H  K  I  M  O  N  O
B  A  N  D  I  T  Y  R  S  E  U  B  X
E  H  S  Z  M  A  G  A  Z  I  N  E  D
C  N  I  O  P  A  J  A  M  A  S  G  I
U  X  J  N  A  V  M  X  K  R  Y  T  V
E  C  T  Y  L  Q  S  O  H  Z  R  A  N
W  U  K  P  A  E  B  E  N  C  U  P  J
S  H  E  I  K  I  Z  T  Q  L  P  O  R
```

1. an outlaw   _____

2. a thick-skinned reptile   _____

3. a backyard cooker   _____

4. worn under a bathrobe   _____

5. sometimes comes from maple trees   _____

6. a weekly or monthly publication   _____

7. an antelope's relative   _____

8. loose clothing worn with a sash   _____

9. an ingredient in gumbo soup   _____

10. head of a village or tribe   _____

© 240 VOCABULARY WORDS FOR GRADE 5   SCHOLASTIC PROFESSIONAL BOOKS

Clips

coed	taxi	ref	limo	champ
grad	mike	fan	curio	rev

▌ A **CLIP** IS A WORD THAT HAS
BEEN SHORTENED, OR CLIPPED.

A **coed** is a female student at a school for males and females.

A **taxi** is a car for hire.

A **ref** is a judge in a sports event.

A clip for *limousine* is **limo**.

If you're a **champ**, you're a winner.

A **grad** is a student who has earned a diploma at a school.

When you're a **fan**, you're a supporter of someone.

A **curio** is a strange or novel object.

A **rev** is a rotation.

A **mike** is an instrument
that magnifies sound.

A. Draw a line to match each clip with the word from which it comes.

1. **mike**   **a.** revolution

2. **grad**   **b.** fanatic

3. **ref**   **c.** champion

4. **champ**   **d.** microphone

5. **rev**   **e.** graduate

6. **curio**   **f.** referee

7. **fan**   **g.** curiosity

B. Write the clip for each word.

1. coeducation   2. taxicab   3. limousine

_____   _____   _____

NAME _____ DATE _____

Clips

coed	taxi	ref	limo	champ
grad	mike	fan	curio	rev

A. Use what you know. Write the best word for each sentence.

1. The _____ called a foul on one of the players.

2. Grace is a _____ at the state university.

3. My aunt was driven to her wedding in a white _____ .

4. The explorer brought back a _____ from her travels.

5. The speaker used a _____ so everyone could hear her.

6. Some _____ students came back to the campus for a reunion.

7. When it comes to skating competition, Ali is the _____ .

8. Oscar checked the meter of his _____ as he drove a passenger home.

9. Chris is a big _____ of that band.

10. The _____ of the motor increased as Carl gave it more gas.

B. Read each question. Choose the best answer.

1. Which one is a person?   ❏ mike   ❏ fan   ❏ rev

2. Which one provides a service?   ❏ taxi   ❏ curio   ❏ champ

3. Which one makes decisions?   ❏ rev   ❏ ref   ❏ limo

4. What does a singer need?   ❏ hike   ❏ bike   ❏ mike

✎ Writing to Learn

Write a sports story for a newspaper. Use at least three vocabulary words.

© 240 VOCABULARY WORDS FOR GRADE 5   SCHOLASTIC PROFESSIONAL BOOKS

LESSON 10

NAME _____ DATE _____

Clips

Complete a chain for each word. In each circle, write a word that is related to the word just before it. An example is done for you.

fan	follower	enthusiastic	cheering	autograph

1. coed ⬭ ⬭ ⬭ ⬭

2. ref ⬭ ⬭ ⬭ ⬭

3. limo ⬭ ⬭ ⬭ ⬭

4. curio ⬭ ⬭ ⬭ ⬭

5. grad ⬭ ⬭ ⬭ ⬭

6. champ ⬭ ⬭ ⬭ ⬭

7. taxi ⬭ ⬭ ⬭ ⬭

8. mike ⬭ ⬭ ⬭ ⬭

9. rev ⬭ ⬭ ⬭ ⬭

© 240 VOCABULARY WORDS FOR GRADE 5   SCHOLASTIC PROFESSIONAL BOOKS

Blends

splatter	squiggle	squawk	paratroops	flurry
glimmer	medevac	spacelab	telethon	flare

A **BLEND** IS A WORD FORMED WHEN PARTS OF TWO WORDS ARE COMBINED OR BLENDED TOGETHER. A BLEND IS ALSO CALLED A *PORTMANTEAU* WORD. A PORTMANTEAU IS A SUITCASE WITH TWO SIDES.

If you **splatter** something, you spray it around.

A **squiggle** is a twist or curve.

A **squawk** is a loud, harsh sound.

A **flurry** is a sudden gust or movement.

A **glimmer** is a gleam.

A **medevac** is a helicopter for transporting wounded people.

A **spacelab** is a laboratory in space.

A TV program that lasts many hours is a **telethon**.

When something **flares**, it flames up quickly.

Paratroops are military units that use parachutes to descend behind enemy lines.

A. Write the blend formed from each pair of words.

1. squall and squeak _____

2. television and marathon _____

3. splash and spatter _____

4. medical and evacuation _____

5. parachute and troops _____

6. squirm and wiggle _____

7. gleam and shimmer _____

8. flame and glare _____

B. Write the vocabulary word for each clue.

1. I'm a place where research goes on.

   _____

2. I sometimes arrive in the form of snow.

   _____

NAME _____ DATE _____

Blends

splatter	squiggle	squawk	paratroops	flurry
glimmer	medevac	spacelab	telethon	flare

A. Use what you know. Write the best word to complete each sentence.

1. The _____ arrived quickly to pick up the injured soldiers.

2. Scientists aboard the _____ announced some new discoveries today.

3. The driver lit a _____ to show where the disabled car was.

4. A _____ of light from the moon fell across the floor.

5. That _____ was from the hen in the barnyard.

6. Jamal drew a _____ on his notepad during the lecture.

7. Don't _____ paint all over your new shirt when you open the can.

8. Millions of people watched the _____ to raise money for charity.

9. The breeze created a small _____ that rustled the leaves.

10. As they neared the target, the _____ got ready to drop from the plane.

B. Read each question. Choose the best answer.

1. Which one is a noise?   ❏ squawk   ❏ squiggle   ❏ square

2. Which one is a light?   ❏ glance   ❏ glimmer   ❏ glutton

3. What is a medevac for?   ❏ destroy   ❏ resist   ❏ rescue

4. Which one is long?   ❏ telephone   ❏ telethon   ❏ technician

✎ Writing to Learn

Write a communication from a spacelab to control center on Earth. Use at least three vocabulary words.

Blends

Use the clues to complete the puzzle.

Across

1. a sudden outburst
2. a place where observations occur
3. what a parrot does
4. evacuation aircraft
5. a kind of glow
6. a lengthy show
7. highly trained jumpers

Down

1. what a fire does
2. not a straight line
3. a messy sprinkle

Collective Nouns

colony	knot	skulk	company	string
gaggle	school	bed	gang	troop

A **COLLECTIVE NOUN** NAMES A GROUP OF ANIMALS, PEOPLE, OR THINGS. A COLLECTIVE NOUN CAN HAVE A SINGULAR OR PLURAL VERB DEPENDING ON HOW IT IS USED IN A SENTENCE.

Ants live together in a **colony**.

When you see a group of toads, they're in a **knot**.

Foxes are found together in a **skulk**.

A group of ponies is called a **string**.

A group of geese on water is a **gaggle**.

A group of fish is called a **school**.

Oysters live in a **bed**.

A **gang** of elk is a group of them.

Kangaroos jump around together in a **troop**.

You'll find parrots together in a **company**.

A. Match each animal to its collective noun.

1. fox   a. **troop**

2. elk   b. **colony**

3. kangaroo   c. **skulk**

4. geese   d. **gang**

5. ant   e. **gaggle**

B. The words for some collective nouns have other meanings. Study the pictures. Write the animal name that has the same group name as the picture name.

1.  _____

2.   _____

3.   _____

4.  _____

5.  _____

Collective Nouns

colony	knot	skulk	company	string
gaggle	school	bed	gang	troop

A. Use what you know. Write the best word to complete each sentence.

1. You have to go to Australia to see a _____ of kangaroos.

2. The divers looked for a _____ of oysters.

3. In the rain forest, a _____ of parrots lives in the trees.

4. A _____ of geese honked as we drove up to the farm.

5. There's a _____ of ants out on the patio.

6. The cowboy led a _____ of ponies across the road.

7. Down by the pond, there's a _____ of toads.

8. A _____ of tuna swam by the boat.

9. Watch out for the _____ of foxes in the woods.

10. We saw a _____ of elk in the mountains out West.

B. Read each question. Choose the best answer.

1. Which group can fly? ☐ colony ☐ knot ☐ gaggle

2. Which group has scales? ☐ skulk ☐ school ☐ string

3. What's found in a bed? ☐ pear ☐ peanut ☐ pearl

4. Which group has a joey? ☐ company ☐ gang ☐ troop

Writing to Learn

Choose one group of animals to research and report on. Include any other special words that refer to the animal, such as words for its young, males, females, and alternative collective nouns.

NAME _____   DATE _____

Collective Nouns

An analogy is a comparison based on how things are related to one another. Complete each of these analogies with a vocabulary word.

1. A cow is to a herd as an elk is to a _____ .

2. A robin is to a flock as a goose is to a _____ .

3. A hornet is to a swarm as an ant is to a _____ .

4. A chicken is to a clutch as a parrot is to a _____ .

5. A wolf is to a pack as a fox is to a _____ .

6. A lion is to a pride as a kangaroo is to a _____ .

7. A frog is to an army as a toad is to a _____ .

8. A donkey is to a pace as a pony is to a _____ .

9. A seal is to a trip as a fish is to a _____ .

10. A whale is to a pod as an oyster is to a _____ .

Content Words: Geography

isthmus	peninsula	strait	delta	oasis
tributary	valley	gorge	plateau	archipelago

▌ SPECIAL WORDS NAME DIFFERENT LANDFORMS AND BODIES OF WATER IN **GEOGRAPHY**.

A **strait** is a narrow channel that connects two larger bodies of water.

An **isthmus** is a narrow strip of land that connects two large areas of land.

A **peninsula** is an area of land that is surrounded by water on three sides.

A **delta** is the dirt and sand that collect at the mouth of a river.

An **oasis** is a fertile place in a desert where there are water, trees, and other plants.

A branch of a river is called a **tributary**. / A **valley** is the land that lies between mountains or hills.

A **gorge** is a deep, narrow valley that often has a stream running through it.

A **plateau** is a large area of high, flat land. / A chain of islands is called an **archipelago**.

A. Write the name for each picture.

1.

_____

2.

_____

hills
3.

_____

4. river mouth

_____

5.

_____

6.

_____

B. Write a vocabulary word for each clue.

1. I'm like a branch but not on a tree trunk. _____

2. It's fun to island-hop through me. _____

3. I'm a good place to stop in the desert. _____

4. Another word for me is *canyon*. _____

NAME _____ DATE _____

Content Words: Geography

isthmus	peninsula	strait	delta	oasis
tributary	valley	gorge	plateau	archipelago

A. Use what you know. Write the best word to complete each sentence.

1. The Cheyenne River is a _____ of the Missouri River.

2. A famous _____ is at the mouth of the Mississippi River.

3. A _____ near the tip of South America is named for Ferdinand Magellan.

4. The Galápagos Islands off South America form an _____ .

5. Spain and Portugal are on a large body of land called a _____ .

6. Napa is a _____ in California that is famous for its grapes.

7. You might see camels at an _____ in the Sahara Desert.

8. The country of Panama forms an _____ between North and South America.

9. The high, flat land of central Mexico is a _____ .

10. A waterfall sometimes descends into a deep _____ .

B. Read each question. Choose the best answer.

1. Which one connects?   ☐ island   ☐ isthmus   ☐ oasis

2. Which one is highest?   ☐ plateau   ☐ valley   ☐ delta

3. Which one flows?   ☐ tribute   ☐ tribune   ☐ tributary

4. What is Florida?   ☐ peninsula   ☐ gorge   ☐ archipelago

Writing to Learn

Use a world map or globe to find real examples of three vocabulary words for landforms or bodies of water. Write a description of each.

Content Words: Geography

Read the clues. Then complete the puzzle.

1. found in a river mouth   _____

2. land between mountains   _____

3. a narrow passage of water   _____

4. higher than a plain and flatter than a hill   _____

5. a land link   _____

6. a string of islands over a wide area   _____

7. an arm of land that extends into the water   _____

8. something like a deep canyon   _____

9. a branch of a river   _____

10. desert destination   _____

      1. ___ **E** ___ ___ ___

      2. ___ **A** ___ ___ ___ ___

      3. ___ ___ **R** ___ ___ ___

      4. ___ ___ ___ **T** ___ ___ ___

      5. ___ ___ ___ **H** ___ ___ ___

      6. ___ ___ ___ ___ ___ **P** ___ ___ ___ ___ ___

  7. ___ ___ ___ ___ ___ ___ ___ ___ **A** ___

      8. ___ ___ **R** ___ ___

      9. **T** ___ ___ ___ ___ ___ ___ ___

      10. ___ ___ **S** ___ ___

Content Words: Poetry

rhyme	meter	simile	couplet	personification
haiku	metaphor	alliteration	onomatopoeia	sonnet

▌ SPECIAL WORDS ARE
USED IN **POETRY**.

When a word imitates the sound of something,
it is called **onomatopoeia.**

Bzzzz.

A word that has the same ending sound as another word is a **rhyme**.

Meter is the arrangement of beats in a line of poetry.

A **simile** uses the words *like* or *as* to compare two unlike things.

A **couplet** is two lines of poetry that usually rhyme.

In **personification**, a human characteristic is given to something that is not human.

A **haiku** is a three-line poem in which there are five, seven, and five syllables per line.

A **metaphor** is a comparison of two unlike things.

The repetition of the first sound of several words in a poem is **alliteration**.

A **sonnet** is a poem with 14 lines written in a certain meter and with a special rhyme scheme.

A. Circle the best word for each example.

1. What do you see? A pig in a tree.   **a.** haiku   **b.** rhyme   **c.** metaphor

2. An emerald is as green as grass.   **a.** simile   **b.** couplet   **c.** rhyme

3. The rain has silver sandals.   **a.** sonnet   **b.** onomatopoeia   **c.** personification

4. The Moon's the North Wind's cookie.   **a.** metaphor   **b.** alliteration   **c.** simile

5. Silly Sally sits on the sidewalk.   **a.** sonnet   **b.** onomatopoeia   **c.** alliteration

6. Clatter, bang boom. Look who's in the room.   **a.** metaphor   **b.** personification   **c.** onomatopoeia

---

B. Write the vocabulary word for each clue.

1. I am a rhythm pattern. _____

2. I'm a twosome. _____

3. Shakespeare wrote many of me. _____

4. I am a poem but do not rhyme. _____

Content Words: Poetry

| rhyme | meter | simile | couplet | personification |
| haiku | metaphor | alliteration | onomatopoeia | sonnet |

A. Use what you know. Write the best word to complete each sentence.

1. A tongue twister is an example of _____ .

2. In her _____ , Jessie used the word *as*.

3. Poets often use _____ to create sounds.

4. Although it only has two lines, a _____ can express a lot.

5. A _____ is a short poem that originated in Japan.

6. By giving the table a voice, Rich used _____ in his poem.

7. Not all poems have _____ ; some are in blank verse.

8. Like music, poetry has a _____ made up of accented and unaccented beats.

9. When you write a _____ , you must include 14 lines.

10. Hunter wrote, "My clothes were a mountain on the floor" as his _____ .

B. Read each question. Choose the best answer.

1. Which one depends on consonants? ❏ alligator   ❏ alliteration   ❏ alliance

2. Which one's a poem?   ❏ sonnet   ❏ solar   ❏ sonic

3. What is "squeak"?   ❏ metaphor   ❏ personification   ❏ onomatopoeia

4. What has 17 syllables?   ❏ couplet   ❏ haiku   ❏ sonnet

Writing to Learn

Write a couplet, haiku, or sonnet of your own.

© 240 VOCABULARY WORDS FOR GRADE 5   SCHOLASTIC PROFESSIONAL BOOKS

Content Words: Poetry

Use the vocabulary words to fill in the map. Then add other poetry words that you know.

Forms of Poetry

1. _____

2. _____

3. _____

Poetry Words

Poetic Devices

6. _____

7. _____

8. _____

9. _____

10. _____

Figures of Speech

4. _____

5. _____

Funny Words

doodad	hodgepodge	chitchat	namby-pamby	fiddlesticks
flabbergast	lollygag	hullabaloo	rapscallion	nitty-gritty

▌ SOME WORDS ARE FUN TO KNOW AND USE BECAUSE THEY SOUND OR LOOK **FUNNY**.

A **hodgepodge** is a big mess.

Chitchat is friendly or idle talk.

Someone who is **namby-pamby** is lacking in strength.

Fiddlesticks means "nonsense."

If you **flabbergast** people, you surprise them.

When you **lollygag**, you while away time.

A loud disturbance is a **hullabaloo**.

A **rapscallion** is a scamp. / **Nitty-gritty** is something essential.

Her hat has a fancy ornament called a **doodad**.

A. Read the words in each row. Cross out one word that does not have a similar meaning to the vocabulary word.

1. **hodgepodge**	jumble	hogwash	disorder
2. **rapscallion**	ragtime	rascal	rogue
3. **flabbergast**	astonish	amaze	flatter
4. **namby-pamby**	weak	insipid	naughty
5. **lollygag**	lollipop	fritter	dillydally
6. **doodad**	gewgaw	doodle	object
7. **hullabaloo**	commotion	uproar	humor
8. **chitchat**	chimpanzee	gossip	rumor

B. Read the words in each row. Write a vocabulary word that means almost the same thing.

1. foolishness, rubbish, _____

2. important, core, _____

Funny Words

doodad	**hodgepodge**	**chitchat**	**namby-pamby**	**fiddlesticks**
flabbergast	**lollygag**	**hullabaloo**	**rapscallion**	**nitty-gritty**

A. Use what you know. Write the best word to complete each sentence.

1. Delia thought the main character was weak and rather _____ .

2. Mrs. Perez wished her son would help out and not _____ in his room all day.

3. Grandma has some kind of _____ on her dresser.

4. Nelson does not like us to _____ and make noise when he is reading the paper.

5. When the cat knocked over the garbage can, there was such a _____ !

6. That puppy is nothing but trouble; he's a little _____ .

7. That trick will _____ the unsuspecting audience.

8. Jake's room is a _____ of junk.

9. Let's get to the _____ of the problem.

10. Dad said, " _____ , kids! There's no one under the bed."

B. Read each question. Choose the best answer.

1. Which one's namby-pamby?   ❑ hero   ❑ weakling   ❑ leader

2. What might a rapscallion cause?   ❑ hullabaloo   ❑ horoscope   ❑ honeycomb

3. Why might you lollygag?   ❑ energetic   ❑ busy   ❑ lazy

4. Which one's a messy drawer?   ❑ tidy   ❑ hodgepodge   ❑ empty

Writing to Learn

Write some chitchat that two people might share. Use at least three vocabulary words.

Funny Words

Play a game of Move On. Find a word in the first box that does not have the same meaning as the other three words. Move that word to the next box by writing it on the blank line. Continue until you reach the last box. Complete the sentence in that box.

Start here.

object
article
hodgepodge
doodad

_____
disorder
rapscallion
jumble

chitchat
scamp
_____
troublemaker

Words
are the
_____
of communication.

talk
gossip
hullabaloo
_____

wishy-washy
_____
weak
nitty-gritty

racket
_____
clamor
flabbergast

namby-pamby
silliness
nonsense
_____

tarry
_____
waste
fiddlesticks

_____
astound
lollygag
surprise

Latin Roots *ped, numer, liber*

pedal	pedestal	numeral	enumerate	liberal
pedestrian	biped	numerous	numerator	liberty

MANY WORDS HAVE
LATIN ROOTS.

A **pedestrian** is someone
who goes on foot.

Root:

Ped means "foot."

A **pedal** is a lever worked by a foot.

A **pedestal** is a base on which a statue stands.

A **biped** is an animal with two feet.

Numer means "number."

A **numeral** is a word or letter that stands for
a number.

Numerous means "a great many."

When you **enumerate** something, you go over it step by step.

A **numerator** is the number above the line in a fraction.

Liber means "free."

Liberal means "giving freely."

Liberty is freedom.

A. Read each word. Write the word(s)
from the box that mean the same
thing.

restate	walker	plenty
support	generous	foot bar

1. **numerous** _____

2. **enumerate** _____

3. **pedestrian** _____

4. **pedestal** _____

5. **liberal** _____

6. **pedal** _____

B. Write a vocabulary word
for each picture.

1.

2.

_____   _____

3. $\dfrac{3}{4}$

4. **XXV**

_____   _____

Latin Roots *ped, numer, liber*

pedal	pedestal	numeral	enumerate	liberal
pedestrian	biped	numerous	numerator	liberty

A. Use what you know. Write the best word to complete each sentence.

1. Can Selma _____ all 50 states?

2. The American people are proud of their tradition of _____ .

3. The mosquitoes were so _____ that we ran inside.

4. The _____ waited for the light before crossing.

5. What is the _____ of this fraction?

6. Hakim was a _____ giver and helped many organizations.

7. A bird is an example of a _____ .

8. The driver stepped on the gas _____ so he wouldn't be late.

9. Brent admired the sculpture on its marble _____ .

10. The ancient Mayans used a _____ system of dots and dashes.

B. Read each question. Choose the best answer.

1. Which one do you move? ❑ pedestal   ❑ pedicure   ❑ pedal

2. Which one is a biped? ❑ hawk   ❑ hippo   ❑ horse

3. Which one's for pedestrians? ❑ sideburn   ❑ sideline   ❑ sidewalk

4. What is seven? ❑ numerous   ❑ nuisance   ❑ numeral

✏ Writing to Learn

Explain why it is helpful to know the root of a word. Use at least three vocabulary words as your examples.

LESSON 16   NAME _____   DATE _____

Latin Roots *ped, numer, liber*

Read the clues. Then complete the puzzle.

1. ample   _____

2. used to make a bicycle move   _____

3. a holder for a statue   _____

4. a two-footed creature   _____

5. to count out   _____

6. used in zip codes   _____

7. several or more   _____

8. above a denominator   _____

9. independence   _____

10. someone who strides   _____

```
1.    L  __ __ __ __ __ __
2.  __ __ __  A  __
3. __ __ __ __ __  T  __ __
4.   __  I  __ __ __
5.  __  N  __ __ __ __ __ __ __ __
6. __ __ __ __ __  R  __ __
7. __ __ __ __ __  O  __ __
8. __ __ __ __ __ __  O  __ __ __ __ __
9. __ __ __ __ __  T  __
10. __ __ __ __ __  S  __ __ __ __ __
```

© 240 VOCABULARY WORDS FOR GRADE 5   SCHOLASTIC PROFESSIONAL BOOKS

Latin Roots *clar, dict*

clarity	clarify	clarion	predict	diction
declare	declaration	dictate	dictator	dictionary

MANY WORDS HAVE LATIN ROOTS.

A **dictionary** is a book of alphabetized words, their meanings, and pronunciations.

Root:

Clar means "clear."

Clarity is clearness.

When you **declare** something, you make it known.

If you **clarify** something, you make it clear.

A **declaration** is an announcement.

A **clarion** is a clear, shrill sound.

Dict means "say."

If you **dictate** something, you say it aloud for someone to write down.

When you **predict** something, you say what will happen next.

A **dictator** is a person who rules with total authority.

Diction is a person's manner of speaking.

A. Read the vocabulary word. Find and circle two other words that mean almost the same thing.

1. **diction**	wording	phrasing	opinion
2. **clarify**	interpret	inquire	explain
3. **predict**	prevent	foretell	prophesy
4. **declare**	proclaim	announce	demand
5. **clarity**	obviousness	hidden	clearness
6. **declaration**	statement	delay	proclamation
7. **dictator**	ruler	despot	citizen

B. Underline the root in each word.

1. **clarion**   2. **dictate**   3. **dictionary**

NAME _____ DATE _____

Latin Roots *clar, dict*

clarity	clarify	clarion	predict	diction
declare	declaration	dictate	dictator	dictionary

A. Use what you know. Write the best word to complete each sentence.

1. In this scene, the prince will _____ his love for the princess.

2. If you don't know a word's definition, use a _____ .

3. Nat practiced his _____ before giving his talk to the group.

4. The children can _____ stories to go with their drawings.

5. All the weather reports for tomorrow _____ patchy fog with periods of rain.

6. The article said that the _____ had clamped down on civil rights.

7. The _____ of light and color in that painting is remarkable.

8. This _____ states that school will close early on Friday.

9. The trumpet sounded a _____ call to begin the race.

10. A member of the audience asked the speaker to _____ his statement.

B. Read each question. Choose the best answer.

1. Which one's a reference? ❐ dictator ❐ diction ❐ dictionary

2. Why might you clarify? ❐ secret ❐ clarity ❐ cleverness

3. What can you predict? ❐ past ❐ present ❐ future

4. Which one can you hear? ❐ clarion ❐ clam ❐ clay

Writing to Learn

Write a prediction about something you think will happen. Use at least two vocabulary words.

NAME _____   DATE _____

Latin Roots *clar, dict*

Write the vocabulary word for each clue. Then write the circled letters on the correct numbered lines at the bottom of the page to answer the riddle.

WHERE CAN YOU ALWAYS FIND MONEY?

1. make something apparent   __ __ __ __ __ __ (__)

2. a word book   __ (__) __ __ __ __ __ __ __

3. how you speak   __ __ __ __ __ (__) __

4. to state something   __ __ __ (__) __ __ __

5. make a kind of guess   __ __ __ __ __ __ (__)

6. an authoritative figure   __ __ __ __ __ __ (__) __

7. sound of a battle horn   __ __ __ (__) __ __

8. lucidity   __ __ (__) __ __ __ __

9. a decree   __ __ __ (__) __ __ __ __ __ __ __

10. read aloud for a typist   __ (__) __ __ __ __

__ __ __ __ __ __ __ __ __ __
10   2   9   5   7   6   3   8   4   1

© 240 VOCABULARY WORDS FOR GRADE 5   SCHOLASTIC PROFESSIONAL BOOKS

Greek Word Parts *mech, meter, path*

mechanic	**diameter**	**thermometer**	**speedometer**	**sympathy**
mechanize	**barometer**	**kilometer**	**pathetic**	**pathology**

▌ MANY ENGLISH WORDS HAVE
GREEK WORD PARTS.

A **diameter** is a straight line that
goes through the center of a circle.

Greek Word Part:

Mech means "machine."   A **mechanic** is someone who repairs machines.

Mechanize means "to do by machine."

Meter means "measure."   A **barometer** measures the pressure of the atmosphere.

A **thermometer** measures temperature.

A **kilometer** is a measure of length in the metric system.

A **speedometer** measures how fast a vehicle is going.

Path means "suffer."   **Pathetic** means "pitiful."

When you feel **sympathy**, you feel sorry for someone.

The study of disease is called **pathology**.

A. Draw a line to match each description with the correct vocabulary word.

1. the field of a pathologist   **a.** thermometer

2. a shorter measurement than a mile   **b.** mechanic

3. someone who can fix a car   **c.** diameter

4. what you show for a sad friend   **d.** speedometer

5. a hot and cold measuring instrument   **e.** kilometer

6. helps drivers keep to the speed limit   **f.** pathology

7. a line segment dividing a circle into halves **g.** sympathy

---

B. Underline the Greek word part in each word.

1. **pathetic**   2. **mechanize**   3. **barometer**

Greek Word Parts *mech, meter, path*

mechanic	diameter	thermometer	speedometer	sympathy
mechanize	barometer	kilometer	pathetic	pathology

A. Use what you know. Write the best word to complete each sentence.

1. With her torn dress and dirty face, the child was _____ .

2. A machine can _____ the work in a factory.

3. In health care, _____ is an important field.

4. Betty got a lot of _____ when she broke her arm.

5. The _____ of Earth is about 8,000 miles.

6. There are 1000 meters in a _____ .

7. When a _____ shows low pressure, it means cloudy weather.

8. As we drove home, Mom checked the _____ from time to time.

9. A look at the _____ told the nurse that the man had a high temperature.

10. The _____ arrived to repair the washing machine.

B. Read each question. Choose the best answer.

1. Who needs sympathy?   ❏ winner   ❏ loser   ❏ spectator

2. Who studies pathology?   ❏ doctor   ❏ mechanic   ❏ teacher

3. Who needs a thermometer?   ❏ visitor   ❏ patient   ❏ messenger

4. What does a meteorologist use?   ❏ barometer   ❏ kilometer   ❏ diameter

Writing to Learn

Explain how three of the vocabulary words are formed.

Greek Word Parts *mech, meter, path*

Use the clues to complete the puzzle.

Across:

2. woeful

4. motorize

5. the abbreviation is km

7. compassion

9. a measuring instrument for temperature

Down:

1. people who know how machines work

2. examination of illness

3. a speed reader

6. twice the radius of a circle

8. pressure gauge

Acronyms

scuba	radar	modem	quasar	canola
zip	sonar	laser	snafu	veep

▌ AN **ACRONYM** IS A WORD MADE
FROM THE FIRST LETTERS OF A PHRASE.

Scuba gear enables a diver to breathe underwater.

Radar is an instrument that uses radio waves to determine the distance, direction, and speed of unseen objects.

A **modem** is a device that converts communications signals.

A heavenly object that lets off a blue light and radio waves is a **quasar**.

Canola is a kind of oil used for cooking.

Sonar is a device that uses sound waves to locate objects underwater.

A **laser** produces a strong, narrow beam of light.

If something turns into a big disorganized mess, it's a **snafu**.

A **veep** is a vice president.

A **zip** code is a way of identifying places in the United States for mail delivery.

A. Draw a line to match each phrase to the correct acronym.

1. radio detecting and ranging   **a.** quasar

2. modulator and demodulator   **b.** zip

3. Canada oil—low acid   **c.** laser

4. sound navigation ranging   **d.** snafu

5. self-contained underwater breathing apparatus   **e.** radar

6. light amplification by stimulated emission of radiation   **f.** modem

7. quasi stellar   **g.** canola

8. zone improvement plan   **h.** scuba

9. situation normal all fouled up   **i.** sonar

B. What word do the letters V.P. spell? _____

© 240 VOCABULARY WORDS FOR GRADE 5   SCHOLASTIC PROFESSIONAL BOOKS

NAME _____ DATE _____

Acronyms

scuba	radar	modem	quasar	canola
zip	sonar	laser	snafu	veep

A. Use what you know. Write the best word to complete each sentence.

1. A _____ is larger than a star, but smaller than a galaxy.

2. Don't forget the _____ code when you address a letter.

3. The doctor used a _____ beam to cut away the diseased tissue.

4. A ship's _____ can spot other ships and prevent collisions.

5. The chef used _____ oil on the salad.

6. A submarine uses _____ to guide it as it descends below water surface.

7. Miles was promoted to be the _____ of his division.

8. Carefully, the diver checked her _____ equipment before using it.

9. The storm caused a huge _____ in the plans for the parade.

10. Be sure your _____ is working when you send e-mail.

B. Read each question. Choose the best answer.

1. Which one is liquid? ❑ candy ❑ canola ❑ caramel

2. Which one is numbers? ❑ zinc ❑ zipper ❑ zip

3. Which one's a problem? ❑ sonar ❑ scuba ❑ snafu

4. Which one's a leader? ❑ veep ❑ veil ❑ vein

✍ Writing to Learn

Write a science fiction story. Use at least three vocabulary words.

NAME _____ DATE _____

Acronyms

> **Read the clues. Write the word next to the clue. Then find and circle each word in the puzzle.**
>
> **1.** an underwater breathing tank _____
>
> **2.** a yellow vegetable oil _____
>
> **3.** second in command _____
>
> **4.** sound wave equipment _____
>
> **5.** a postal sorting system _____
>
> **6.** radio wave equipment _____
>
> **7.** a powerful light beam _____
>
> **8.** a computer has one _____
>
> **9.** seen through a telescope _____
>
> **10.** a botched situation _____
>
>
> | S | W | H | S | B | E | J | X | A | C | V |
> |---|---|---|---|---|---|---|---|---|---|---|
> | C | A | N | O | L | A | T | Q | R | K | E |
> | U | C | F | N | M | P | D | S | N | G | E |
> | B | V | D | A | F | Y | L | B | Z | I | P |
> | A | U | J | R | A | D | A | R | A | Q | W |
> | E | N | Z | G | W | C | S | X | G | U | I |
> | M | X | Q | M | O | D | E | M | L | A | R |
> | T | V | S | I | L | B | R | O | T | S | H |
> | D | K | Y | M | N | X | K | E | C | A | A |
> | S | N | A | F | U | V | O | J | Z | R | F |

British English

pram	larder	flat	underground	chemist
lift	cupboard	holiday	nappy	cutlery

SOME **ENGLISH WORDS** HAVE DIFFERENT MEANINGS IN **BRITAIN** THAN THEY DO IN THE UNITED STATES.

A **pram** is a baby carriage.

A **larder** is a pantry.

If you rent a **flat**, you rent an apartment.

The **underground** is a subway.

A **chemist** is a druggist.

If you ride in a **lift**, you take an elevator.

A **cupboard** is a closet.

A diaper is called a **nappy** by the British.

When you set the table with **cutlery**, you use silverware.

When you go on **holiday**, you take a vacation.

A. Write a vocabulary word for each picture.

1.

_____

2.

_____

3.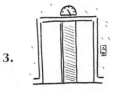

_____

4.

_____

5.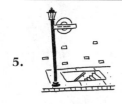

_____

6.

_____

B. Read the words in each row. Write the vocabulary word that means the same thing.

1. storeroom, pantry _____

2. carriage, buggy _____

3. recess, vacation _____

4. pharmacist, druggist _____

British English

pram	larder	flat	underground	chemist
lift	cupboard	holiday	nappy	cutlery

A. Use what you know. Write the best word to complete each sentence.

1. Mother brought an extra _____ for the baby when we went out.

2. Harriet looked in the _____ for something to eat.

3. A customer called the _____ to get his prescription filled.

4. The commuters took the _____ to get to their jobs.

5. Will the Marks take their dog when they go on _____ ?

6. Push the button for the _____ if you're going to the tenth floor.

7. Olivia placed _____ on the table for lunch.

8. Mrs. Elliot put the infant in the _____ so she could go for a walk.

9. The doors to the _____ were open and clothes spilled out.

10. Malcolm rented a _____ for the year he would live in London.

B. Read each question. Choose the best answer.

1. Which one can you ride? ☐ underneath ☐ underweight ☐ underground

2. Which one's for a baby? ☐ prom ☐ prim ☐ pram

3. Which one moves vertically? ☐ sift ☐ lift ☐ rift

4. Which one's for living? ☐ float ☐ flit ☐ flat

✏ Writing to Learn

Write an e-mail message from a British pen pal to one in America. Use at least three vocabulary words.

British English

Complete the chart by adding the missing word or words under each heading.
The first one is done for you.

American Word	British Word	Another Meaning for British Word
1. elevator	**lift**	raise up
2. silverware	_____	cutting instrument
3. apartment	**flat**	_____
4. closet	_____	cabinet
5. _____	**nappy**	a shallow dish
6. _____	**underground**	beneath Earth's surface
7. pantry	_____	a kind of beetle
8. druggist	**chemist**	_____
9. baby carriage	_____	small rowboat
10. _____	**holiday**	day of celebration

Word Stories

album	ketchup	leotard	cyclone	dahlia
oxygen	manuscript	academy	zany	volcano

▌ MANY WORDS HAVE INTERESTING **STORIES** ABOUT THEIR ORIGIN.

If someone is **zany**, that person is clownish.

An **album** is a book with blank pages for holding photos or other collections.

Ketchup is a tomato sauce. / A **leotard** is a bodysuit that dancers wear.

A **cyclone** is a violent, rotating windstorm. / A **dahlia** is a kind of flower.

Oxygen is a colorless gas in the air that people, animals, and plants need to breathe.

Manuscript is the text of a book or paper. / An **academy** is a school.

A **volcano** is a cone-shaped mountain that is formed by lava erupting from a crack in Earth's surface.

A. Write a vocabulary word for each word story.

1. The Greek word *kyklos* refers to a circle.   _____

2. The Italian word *zanni* means a clown.   _____

3. In ancient Rome, public notices were posted on blank tablets named from the Latin word *albus*, meaning "white."   _____

4. The Greek philosopher Plato taught students in a grove called Akadçmeia.   _____

5. Long ago, people in China made a pickled fish sauce called ke-tsiap.   _____

6. Two Latin words, *manu* and *scriptus*, mean "hand" and "write."   _____

B. Draw a line from each vocabulary word to the person associated with the word.

1. oxygen   **a.** Vulcan was the Roman god of fire.

2. volcano   **b.** Anders Dahl was a Swedish botanist in the 1700s.

3. leotard   **c.** French chemist Antoine Laurent Lavoisier first used this word after an important element was identified in the 18th century.

4. dahlia   **d.** Jules Léotard was a French tightrope walker.

NAME _____ DATE _____

Word Stories

album	**ketchup**	**leotard**	**cyclone**	**dahlia**
oxygen	**manuscript**	**academy**	**zany**	**volcano**

A. Use what you know. Write the best word to complete each sentence.

1. The forecaster warned of a _____ forming over the ocean.

2. Tito graduated from the _____ at the head of his class.

3. Ruth wore a black _____ when she took the exercise class.

4. Mt. St. Helen's is an active _____ in Washington State.

5. Without enough _____ , a plant will die.

6. Carmen added _____ to her shopping list for the barbecue.

7. The cast gave a _____ performance that made the audience laugh.

8. At the botanical gardens, we saw some beautiful _____ .

9. Mrs. Quinn keeps an _____ with pictures of family outings.

10. Logan reread his _____ before sending it to the publisher.

B. Read each question. Choose the best answer.

1. Which one seasons?   ❏ ketchup   ❏ ketch   ❏ kettle

2. Which one's essential?   ❏ volcano   ❏ cyclone   ❏ oxygen

3. Which one opens?   ❏ alert   ❏ alarm   ❏ album

4. Which one needs oxygen?   ❏ dahlia   ❏ leotard   ❏ manuscript

Writing to Learn

Find out more about the story behind one of the vocabulary words. Write a short report to explain its background.

NAME _____   DATE _____

Word Stories

Read each list of words. Write a vocabulary word to go with each group.

1. foolish

   clownish

   loony

   _____

2. edit

   write

   revise

   _____

3. tornado

   typhoon

   damage

   _____

4. spicy

   hamburger

   reddish

   _____

5. mountain

   lava

   eruption

   _____

6. garden

   water

   blossom

   _____

7. stamp

   autograph

   wedding

   _____

8. gymnast

   acrobat

   dancer

   _____

9. school

   college

   university

   _____

10. nitrogen

   carbon

   hydrogen

   _____

NAME _____   **DATE** _____

Prefixes *retro-, ir-, mal-, inter-, ab-*

retroactive	**ir**responsible	**mal**function	**inter**section	**ab**duct
retrospective	**ir**rational	**mal**formed	**inter**pose	**ab**stain

▎ A **PREFIX** IS A WORD PART THAT HAS BEEN ADDED TO THE BEGINNING
OF A WORD AND CHANGES THE WORD'S MEANING.

retro- means "backward"
ir- means "not"
mal- means "bad"
inter- means "between"
ab- means "from"

If something **malfunctions**,
it doesn't work.

A law that is **retroactive** applies to events before the law was passed.

A **retrospective** is a survey of past experiences.

If you are **irresponsible**, you are not responsible.

When someone is **irrational**, that person is not thinking clearly.

Malformed means "poorly shaped." / An **intersection** is where one thing crosses another.

To **interpose** means "to come between things." / **Abduct** means "carry off by force."

If you **abstain** from something, you do without it.

**A. Read the words in each row. Write
a vocabulary word that means
almost the same thing.**

1. unreliable, untrustworthy _____

2. refrain, forego _____

3. intervene, insert _____

4. distorted, misshapen _____

5. seize, kidnap _____

6. illogical, unreasonable _____

**B. Add the correct prefix to each word
to form a new word. Use the meaning clue in parentheses to help you.**

1. (backward) _____active

2. (between) _____section

3. (bad) _____function

4. (backward) _____spective

Prefixes *retro-, ir-, mal-, inter-, ab-*

retroactive	**ir**responsible	**mal**function	**inter**section	**ab**duct
retrospective	**ir**rational	**mal**formed	**inter**pose	**ab**stain

A. Use what you know. Write the best word to complete each sentence.

1. Bria found it very hard to _____ from chocolate.

2. That tree has a _____ and twisted trunk.

3. To reach the library, turn right at the next _____ .

4. In the story, a dragon tries to _____ the princess.

5. There will be a _____ of the artist's work at the gallery next week.

6. Ming tried to _____ her ideas into the conversation.

7. It was _____ of Ryan to leave your bike out all night.

8. Let's hope the washing machine doesn't _____ because we have a lot of laundry.

9. Heavy traffic can make some drivers upset and _____ .

10. The tax increase will be _____ to the first of the year.

B. Read each question. Choose the best answer.

1. Which one's an intersection?   ❑ circle   ❑ curve   ❑ cross

2. What does a dieter do?   ❑ abduct   ❑ abstain   ❑ absurd

3. What can malfunction?   ❑ rock   ❑ rocket   ❑ rocky

4. When might you intervene?   ❑ fight   ❑ field   ❑ fiction

✍ Writing to Learn

Explain how a prefix changes the meaning of a word. Use at least three vocabulary words as examples.

Prefixes *retro-, ir-, mal-, inter-, ab-*

Underline the prefix in each word below. Use what you know about the prefix meaning to write the meaning of the word. Check your answers in a dictionary.

1. interstate _____

_____

2. irregular _____

_____

3. malcontent _____

_____

4. abnormal _____

_____

5. irreverence _____

_____

6. absent _____

_____

7. interdependence _____

_____

8. retrovirus _____

_____

9. malnutrition _____

_____

10. retro-rocket _____

_____

NAME _____ DATE _____

Prefixes *bi-, com-, il-, hydro-, mono-*

bivalve	commiserate	illegal	hydroplane	monotone
biannual	compile	illiterate	hydroelectric	monosyllable

A **PREFIX** IS A WORD PART THAT HAS BEEN ADDED TO THE BEGINNING OF A WORD AND CHANGES THE WORD'S MEANING.

bi- means "two"
com- means "with"
il- means "not"
hydro- means "water"
mono- means "single"

A **bivalve** is a shell with two parts that hinge together.

A **biannual** event occurs twice a year.

If you **commiserate** with someone, you feel sorrow for his or her trouble.

When you **compile** things, you collect them. / Something that is **illegal** is against the law.

A person who does not know how to read or write is **illiterate**.

A **hydroplane** can land or take off on water. / Electricity made from waterpower is **hydroelectric.**

Monotone means "sameness of tone or style." / A **monosyllable** is a word with one syllable.

A. Read each word. Write the word from the box that means almost the same thing.

compile	commiserate
illiterate	illegal
monotone	hydroplane

1. unlearned _____

2. seaplane _____

3. pity _____

4. unlawful _____

5. assemble _____

6. drone _____

B. Add the correct prefix to each word to form a new word. Use the meaning clue in parentheses to help you.

1. (two) _____valve

2. (single) _____syllable

3. (water) _____electric

4. (two) _____annual

NAME _____   DATE _____

Prefixes *bi-, com-, il-, hydro-, mono-*

bivalve	**com**miserate	**il**legal	**hydro**plane	**mono**tone
biannual	**com**pile	**il**literate	**hydro**electric	**mono**syllable

A. Use what you know. Write the best word to complete each sentence.

1. Cody will _____ a list of names for the party.

2. The reporter expected more than a _____ when she asked the candidate a question.

3. That dam provides _____ power for much of the state.

4. Our school has a _____ picnic, once in the fall and again in the spring.

5. The bathers found a _____ in the sand at the beach.

6. We _____ with people who lose their homes in disasters like floods.

7. In some cities, it's _____ to make a right turn on a red light.

8. The speaker was very boring because he spoke in a _____ .

9. The _____ circled and touched down on the river.

10. People who are _____ have a hard time finding meaningful work.

B. Read each question. Choose the best answer.

1. What do you compile?   ❏ nuts   ❏ notes   ❏ naps

2. Which one is a mollusk?   ❏ biannual   ❏ bivalve   ❏ biography

3. What makes a monotone?   ❏ eyes   ❏ nose   ❏ mouth

4. Which one's a monosyllable? ❏ illiterate   ❏ ill   ❏ illegal

✏ Writing to Learn

Write three newspaper headlines. Use a vocabulary word in each.

LESSON 23

NAME _____ **DATE** _____

Prefixes *bi-, com-, il-, hydro-, mono-*

Play the Word Building game. Add one of the prefixes on the list to the roof of each house. Then write the new word on the sidewalk. Use a dictionary to check your words. On another piece of paper, write a sentence using each new word.

Prefixes: hydro-   il-   com-   bi-   mono-

1. chrome

2. weekly

3. rail

4. press

5. legible

6. meter

7. lingual

8. foil

9. motion

74

© *240 VOCABULARY WORDS FOR GRADE 5*   SCHOLASTIC PROFESSIONAL BOOKS

NAME _____ DATE _____

Suffixes -ist, -ic, -ation/-tion, -ism, -ent

| dentist | heroic | accusation | optimism | turbulent |
| perfectionist | historic | recreation | journalism | succulent |

▌ A **SUFFIX** IS A WORD PART THAT IS ADDED TO THE END
▌ OF A WORD AND CHANGES THE MEANING OF THE WORD.

-ist means "one who practices"
-ic means "relating to"
-ation/-tion and **-ism** mean "state of being"
-ent means 'inclined to"

Recreation is amusement.

A **dentist** is a doctor for teeth.
A **perfectionist** is a person who likes things to be perfect.
Someone who is **heroic** is very brave.
Historic means "famous in history."
An **accusation** is a charge against someone.
Optimism is the belief that things will turn out for the best.
Journalism is the writing and publishing of newspapers and magazines.
When something is **turbulent**, it is disturbed.
Succulent means "juicy."

A. Read the vocabulary word. Find and underline two other words in the row that mean almost the same thing.

1. **accusation**	denouncement	assortment	charge
2. **recreation**	reflection	relaxation	play
3. **heroic**	noble	courageous	horrible
4. **turbulent**	peaceful	disorderly	unruly
5. **historic**	renowned	celebrated	recent
6. **succulent**	juicy	tough	fleshy
7. **optimism**	affection	hopefulness	cheerfulness

B. Underline the suffix in each word.

1. **dentist**   2. **journalism**   3. **perfectionist**

NAME _____ DATE _____

Suffixes -ist, -ic, -ation/-tion, -ism, -ent

| dentist | heroic | accusation | optimism | turbulent |
| perfectionist | historic | recreation | journalism | succulent |

A. Use what you know. Write the best word to complete each sentence.

1. After work, Simon likes to play basketball for _____ .

2. The _____ examined Corey's teeth for cavities.

3. During the storm, the water was choppy and _____ .

4. Our class visited an _____ part of town for a social studies project.

5. Isabel's good spirits and _____ help her get through difficult situations.

6. Matsu hopes to get a job in _____ when she finishes school.

7. Alberto slowly bit into a _____ piece of meat.

8. The student was a _____ who tried to get everything right.

9. The firefighters were _____ in their efforts to rescue people.

10. The _____ against the offender was serious.

B. Read each question. Choose the best answer.

1. Which one is turbulent? ❐ chair   ❐ air   ❐ stair

2. Which one's fun? ❐ delegation   ❐ accusation   ❐ recreation

3. Which one's upbeat? ❐ optimism   ❐ pessimism   ❐ realism

4. What's a peach? ❐ turbulent   ❐ succulent   ❐ tolerant

Writing to Learn

Explain how a suffix changes the meaning of a word. Use at least three vocabulary words as examples.

Suffixes -ist, -ic, -ation/-tion, -ism, -ent

Here's a challenge for you. Write at least four words that end with each suffix.
Use one of the words from each group in a sentence.

1. *-ist*   _____

    _____ _____

    _____ _____

    _____

2. *-ic*   _____

    _____ _____

    _____ _____

    _____

3. *-ation/-tion* _____

    _____ _____

    _____ _____

    _____

4. *-ism*   _____

    _____ _____

    _____ _____

    _____

5. *-ent*   _____

    _____ _____

    _____ _____

    _____

Word List

abduct, p. 69
abstain, p. 69
academy, p. 66
accusation, p. 75
album, p. 66
alligator, p. 30
alliteration, p. 45
allow, p. 12
archipelago, p. 42

bandit, p. 30
barbecue, p. 30
barometer, p. 57
bed, p. 39
bewildered, p. 9
biannual, p. 72
bikini, p. 27
biped, p. 51
bivalve, p. 72
blissful, p. 9
blueprint, p. 18
blunder, p. 6
bologna, p. 27
bountiful, p. 9
bridal, p. 21
bridle, p. 21
brutal, p. 9

canola, p. 60
cantaloupe, p. 27
ceaseless, p. 9
champ, p. 33
chemist, p. 63
chitchat, p. 48
clarify, p. 54
clarion, p. 54
clarity, p. 54
coarse, p. 21
coed, p. 33
cologne, p. 27
colony, p. 39
commiserate, p. 72
company, p. 39
compile, p. 72
compliment, p. 12
considerate, p. 15
couplet, p. 45
course, p. 21
crews, p. 21
criticism, p. 12
cruise, p. 21
cumbersome, p. 9
cupboard, p. 63
curio, p. 33
cutlery, p. 63
cyclone, p. 66

dahlia, p. 66
daunting, p. 9
declaration, p. 54
declare, p. 54
delta, p. 42
dentist, p. 75
diameter, p. 57
dictate, p. 54
dictator, p. 54
diction, p. 54
dictionary, p. 54
doodad, p. 48
dormant, p. 9

earthquake, p. 18
enumerate, p. 51

fan, p. 33
fatigue, p. 12
fiddlesticks, p. 48
flabbergast, p. 48
flare, p. 36
flat, p. 63
flimsy, p. 12
flurry, p. 36
foul, p. 21
fowl, p. 21
frisky, p. 15

gaggle, p. 39
gang, p. 39
generally, p. 6
glimmer, p. 36
gorge, p. 42
grad, p. 33
guidebook, p. 18

haiku, p. 45
hazardous, p. 6
headquarters, p. 18
heedless, p. 15
heroic, p. 75
historic, p. 75
hodgepodge, p. 48
holiday, p. 63
hullabaloo, p. 48
hydroelectric, p. 72
hydroplane, p. 72

illegal, p. 72
illiterate, p. 72
impala, p. 30
interesting, p. 15
interpose, p. 69
intersection, p. 69
invalid, p. 24
invalid, p. 24
irrational, p. 69

irresponsible, p. 69
isthmus, p. 42

journalism, p. 75

ketchup, p. 66
kilometer, p. 57
kimono, p. 30
knot, p. 39

larder, p. 63
laser, p. 60
leotard, p. 66
liberal, p. 51
liberty, p. 51
lift, p. 63
limo, p. 33
lollygag, p. 48
loot, p. 21
lute, p. 21

magazine, p. 30
malformed, p. 69
malfunction, p. 69
manuscript, p. 66
marathon, p. 27
masterpiece, p. 18
mechanic, p. 57
mechanize, p. 57
medevac, p. 36
metaphor, p. 45
meter, p. 45
mike, p. 33
minute, p. 24
minute, p. 24
modem, p. 60
monosyllable, p. 72
monotone, p. 72

namby-pamby, p. 48
nappy, p. 63
nitty-gritty, p. 48
novice, p. 6
numeral, p. 51
numerator, p. 51
numerous, p. 51

oasis, p. 42
object, p. 24
object, p. 24
okra, p. 30
onomatopoeia, p. 45
optimism, p. 75
ordinary, p. 12
outstanding, p. 6
oxygen, p. 66

pajamas, p. 30
paratroops, p. 36
pathetic, p. 57
pathology, p. 57
pedal, p. 51
pedestal, p. 51
pedestrian, p. 51
peninsula, p. 42
perfectionist, p. 75
permanent, p. 15
personification,
   p. 45
plateau, p. 42
pram, p. 63
predict, p. 54
present, p. 24
present, p. 24
prohibit, p. 12

quasar, p. 60
quiver, p. 6

radar, p. 60
rapscallion, p. 48
rash, p. 6
receptacle, p. 6
recreation, p. 75
ref, p. 33
refuse, p. 24
refuse, p. 24
retroactive, p. 69
retrospective, p. 69
rev, p. 33
rhyme, p. 45
ridiculous, p. 15

sardines, p. 27
school, p. 39
scuba, p. 60
sensible, p. 15
sheik, p. 30
simile, p. 45
skulk, p. 39
sluggish, p. 15
snafu, p. 60
sonar, p. 60
sonnet, p. 45
spacelab, p. 36
speedometer, p. 57
spellbound, p. 18
splatter, p. 36
squawk, p. 36
squiggle, p. 36
strait, p. 42
string, p. 39
substantial, p. 12
succulent, p. 75
sympathy, p. 57
syrup, p. 30

tangerine, p. 27
tarantula, p. 27
taxi, p. 33
telethon, p. 36
thermometer, p. 57
tiresome, p. 15
touchdown, p. 18
treacherous, p. 9
tributary, p. 42
troop, p. 39
turbulent, p. 75
tuxedo, p. 27

underground, p. 63
unique, p. 12
unstable, p. 15

valid, p. 9
valley, p. 42
variable, p. 6
vaudeville, p. 27
veep, p. 60
veto, p. 6
vigor, p. 12
vineyard, p. 18
volcano, p. 66

whirlpool, p. 18
windshield, p. 18

zany, p. 66
zip, p. 60

Answers

Lesson 1, page 6: A. 1. tremble, shake, shiver 2. harmful, risky, dangerous 3. newcomer, beginner, learner 4. error, mistake, misjudgment 5. commonly, usually, mostly 6. notable, important, remarkable 7. foolhardy, reckless, careless 8. prohibit, forbid, ban
B. 1. variable 2. receptacle **page 7: A.** 1. outstanding 2. quiver 3. blunder 4. receptacle 5. rash 6. novice 7. veto 8. hazardous 9. generally 10. variable **B.** 1. rookie 2. poison 3. fear 4. bag **page 8:** 1. rash 2. veto 3. receptacle 4. hazardous 5. novice 6. outstanding 7. generally 8. blunder 9. quiver 10. variable
Lesson 2, page 9: A. 1. ceaseless 2. bewildered 3. treacherous 4. blissful 5. daunting 6. bountiful 7. valid 8. brutal **B.** 1. cumbersome 2. dormant **page 10: A.** 1. cumbersome 2. ceaseless 3. valid 4. bountiful 5. daunting 6. treacherous 7. brutal 8. blissful 9. bewildered 10. dormant **B.** 1. bride 2. waterfall 3. beginner 4. feast **page 11:** 1. blissful 2. dormant 3. treacherous 4. bountiful 5. brutal 6. daunting 7. ceaseless 8. cumbersome 9. valid 10. valid
Lesson 3, page 12: A. 1. firm 2. unmatched 3. permit 4. disapproval 5. prevent 6. energy 7. praise 8. weak **B.** 1. exhaustion/vigor 2. usual/unique 3. allow/forbid 4. flimsy/sturdy **page 13: A.** 1. compliment 2. allow 3. vigor 4. ordinary 5. fatigue 6. substantial 7. prohibit 8. criticism 9. unique 10. flimsy **B.** 1. house 2. compliment 3. jumping 4. original **page 14:** compliment, unique, fatigue, allow, substantial
Lesson 4, page 15: A. 1. inactive 2. settled 3. wise 4. boring 5. ridiculous 6. thoughtless **B.** 1. unsettled, stable 2. playful, lazy 3. thoughtful, inconsiderate 4. fascinating, dull
page 16: A. 1. considerate 2. frisky 3. unstable 4. ridiculous 5. sluggish 6. tiresome 7. permanent 8. heedless 9. sensible 10. interesting **B.** 1. frisky 2. ink 3. sluggish 4. waves **page 17:** 1. slow, sluggish, idle 2. absurd, rash, ridiculous

3. impermanent, unstable, interrupted 4. dull, tiresome, uninteresting 5. inattentive, careless, heedless
Lesson 5, page 18: A. 1. windshield 2. guidebook 3. earthquake 4. blueprint 5. vineyard 6. whirlpool 7. masterpiece **B.** 1. head, quarters 2. touch, down 3. spell, bound
page 19: A. 1. headquarters 2. guidebook 3. windshield 4. touchdown 5. vineyard 6. earthquake 7. masterpiece 8. spellbound 9. blueprint 10. whirlpool
B. 1. windshield 2. blueprint 3. quarterback 4. fruit **page 20:** 1. earthquake 2. windshield 3. masterpiece 4. vineyard 5. whirlpool 6. blueprint 7. touchdown 8. headquarters 9. spellbound 10. guidebook. Riddle: a staircase
Lesson 6, page 21: A. 1. bridle 2. lute 3. foul 4. cruise **B.** 1. course 2. coarse **page 22: A.** 1. crews 2. foul 3. bridal 4. cruise 5. coarse 6. lute 7. fowl 8. bridle 9. loot 10. course **B.** 1. fowl 2. groom 3. lute 4. rowers **page 23:** 1. A Bridle for My Horse 2. How to Play the Lute 3. Planning a Course for a Vacation Cruise 4. Foul Play! The Story of Crews that Loot Bridal Parties 5. Tips for Raising Fowl 6. Using Burlap and Other Coarse Fabrics
Lesson 7, page 24: A. 1. a 2. b 3. b 4. b 5. a 6. a **B.** 1. invalid 2. object 3. refuse 4. minute
page 25: A. 1. invalid 2. present 3. invalid 4. minute 5. object 6. refuse 7. minute 8. refuse 9. present 10. object **B.** 1. no 2. yes 3. no 4. no **page 26:** 1. 1 2. 2 3. 1 4. 2 5. 2 6. 1 7. 1 8. 2 9. 1 10. 2
Lesson 8, page 27: A. 1. cantaloupe 2. marathon 3. vaudeville 4. tuxedo 5. cologne 6. sardines **B.** 1. c 2. d 3. b 4. a
page 28: A. 1. cologne 2. marathon 3. bologna 4. tarantula 5. cantaloupe 6. sardines 7. vaudeville 8. tuxedo 9. bikini 10. tangerine **B.** 1. tuxedo 2. marathon 3. tarantula 4. sardine **page 29:** 1. bikini 2. tarantula 3. tangerine 4. cologne 5. tuxedo 6. sardines 7. bologna 8. vaudeville 9. marathon 10. cantaloupe
Lesson 9, page 30: A. 1. Japanese

2. African 3. Arabic 4. Arabic 5. Persian 6. African **B.** 1. magazine 2. alligator 3. sheik 4. barbecues
page 31: A. 1. alligator 2. syrup 3. magazine 4. barbecue 5. pajamas 6. bandit 7. kimono 8. impala 9. okra 10. sheik **B.** 1. pajamas 2. syrup 3. magazine 4. impala
page 32: 1. bandit 2. alligator 3. barbecue 4. pajamas 5. syrup 6. magazine 7. impala 8. kimono 9. okra 10. sheik
Lesson 10, page 33: A. 1. d 2. e 3. f 4. c 5. a 6. g 7. b **B.** 1. coed 2. taxi 3. limo **page 34: A.** 1. ref 2. coed 3. limo 4. curio 5. mike 6. grad 7. champ 8. taxi 9. fan 10. rev **B.** 1. fan 2. taxi 3. ref 4. mike **page 35:** Answers will vary.
Lesson 11, page 36: A. 1. squawk 2. telethon 3. splatter 4. medevac 5. paratroops 6. squiggle 7. glimmer 8. flare **B.** 1. spacelab 2. flurry
page 37: A. 1. medevac 2. spacelab 3. flare 4. glimmer 5. squawk 6. squiggle 7. splatter 8. telethon 9. flurry 10. paratroops
B. 1. squawk 2. glimmer 3. rescue 4. telethon **page 38:** Across: 1. flurry 2. spacelab 3. squawk 4. medevac 5. glimmer 6. telethon 7. paratroops Down: 1. flare 2. squiggle 3. splatter
Lesson 12, page 39: A. 1. c 2. d 3. a 4. e 5. b **B.** 1. toads 2. oysters 3. ponies 4. fish 5. parrots **page 40: A.** 1. troop 2. bed 3. company 4. gaggle 5. colony 6. string 7. knot 8. school 9. skulk 10. gang **B.** 1. gaggle 2. school 3. pearl 4. troop
page 41: 1. gang 2. gaggle 3. colony 4. company 5. skulk 6. troop 7. knot 8. string 9. school 10. bed
Lesson 13, page 42: A. 1. peninsula 2. strait 3. valley 4. delta 5. plateau 6. isthmus **B.** 1. tributary 2. archipelago 3. oasis 4. gorge
page 43: A. 1. tributary 2. delta 3. strait 4. archipelago 5. peninsula 6. valley 7. oasis 8. isthmus 9. plateau 10. gorge **B.** 1. isthmus 2. plateau 3. tributary 4. peninsula
page 44: 1. delta 2. valley 3. strait 4. plateau 5. isthmus 6. archipelago 7. peninsula 8. gorge 9. tributary 10. oasis
Lesson 14, page 45: A. 1. b 2. a

3. c 4. a 5. c 6. c **B.** 1. meter 2. couplet 3. sonnet 4. haiku **page 46:** **A.** 1. alliteration 2. simile 3. onomatopoeia 4. couplet 5. haiku 6. personification 7. rhyme 8. meter 9. sonnet 10. metaphor **B.** 1. alliteration 2. sonnet 3. onomatopoeia 4. haiku **page 47:** Forms: 1. haiku 2. couplet 3. sonnet Figures: 4. simile 5. metaphor Devices: 6. rhyme 7. meter 8. personification 9. alliteration 10. onomatopoeia

Lesson 15, page 48: A. 1. hogwash 2. ragtime 3. flatter 4. naughty 5. lollipop 6. doodle 7. humor 8. chimpanzee **B.** 1. fiddlesticks 2. nitty-gritty **page 49: A.** 1. namby-pamby 2. lollygag 3. doodad 4. chitchat 5. hullabaloo 6. rapscallion 7. flabbergast 8. hodgepodge 9. nitty-gritty 10. Fiddlesticks **B.** 1. weakling 2. hullabaloo 3. lazy 4. hodgepodge **page 50:** 1. hodgepodge 2. rapscallion 3. chitchat 4. hullabaloo 5. flabbergast 6. lollygag 7. fiddlesticks 8. namby-pamby 9. nitty-gritty 10. nitty-gritty

Lesson 16, page 51: A. 1. plenty 2. restate 3. walker 4. support 5. generous 6. foot bar **B.** 1. biped 2. liberty 3. numerator 4. numeral **page 52: A.** 1. enumerate 2. liberty 3. numerous 4. pedestrian 5. numerator 6. liberal 7. biped 8. pedal 9. pedestal 10. numeral **B.** 1. pedal 2. hawk 3. sidewalk 4. numeral **page 53:** 1. liberal 2. pedal 3. pedestal 4. biped 5. enumerate 6. numeral 7. numerous 8. numerator 9. liberty 10. pedestrian

Lesson 17, page 54: A. 1. wording, phrasing 2. interpret, explain 3. foretell, prophesy 4. proclaim, announce 5. obviousness, clearness 6. statement, proclamation 7. ruler, despot **B.** 1. clarion 2. dictate 3. dictionary **page 55: A.** 1. declare 2. dictionary 3. diction 4. dictate 5. predict 6. dictator 7. clarity 8. declaration 9. clarion 10. clarify **B.** 1. dictionary 2. clarity 3. future 4. clarion **page 56:** 1. clarify 2. dictionary 3. diction 4. declare 5. predict 6. dictator 7. clarion 8. clarity 9. declaration 10. dictate Riddle: dictionary

Lesson 18, page 57: A. 1. f 2. e 3. b 4. g 5. a 6. d 7. c **B.** 1. pathetic

2. mechanize 3. barometer **page 58: A.** 1. pathetic 2. mechanize 3. pathology 4. sympathy 5. diameter 6. kilometer 7. barometer 8. speedometer 9. thermometer 10. mechanic **B.** 1. loser 2. doctor 3. patient 4. barometer **page 59:** Across: 2. pathetic 4. mechanize 5. kilometer 7. sympathy 9. thermometer Down: 1. mechanics 2. pathology 3. speedometer 6. diameter 8. barometer

Lesson 19, page 60: A. 1. e 2. f 3. g 4. i 5. h 6. c 7. a 8. b 9. d **B.** veep **page 61: A.** 1. quasar 2. zip 3. laser 4. radar 5. canola 6. sonar 7. veep 8. scuba 9. snafu 10. modem **B.** 1. canola 2. zip 3. snafu 4. veep **page 62:** 1. scuba 2. canola 3. veep 4. sonar 5. zip 6. radar 7. laser 8. modem 9. quasar 10. snafu

Lesson 20, page 63: A. 1. cutlery 2. flat 3. lift 4. cupboard 5. underground 6. nappy **B.** 1. larder 2. pram 3. holiday 4. chemist **page 64: A.** 1. nappy 2. larder 3. chemist 4. underground 5. holiday 6. lift 7. cutlery 8. pram 9. cupboard 10. flat **B.** 1. underground 2. pram 3. lift 4. flat **page 65:** 2. cutlery 3. opposite of bumpy 4. cupboard 5. diaper 6. subway 7. larder 8. scientist 9. pram 10. vacation

Lesson 21, page 66: A. 1. cyclone 2. zany 3. album 4. academy 5. ketchup 6. manuscript **B.** 1. c 2. a 3. d 4. b **page 67: A.** 1. cyclone 2. academy 3. leotard 4. volcano 5. oxygen 6. ketchup 7. zany 8. dahlias 9. album 10. manuscript **B.** 1. ketchup 2. oxygen 3. album 4. dahlia **page 68:** 1. zany 2. manuscript 3. cyclone 4. ketchup 5. volcano 6. dahlia 7. album 8. leotard 9. academy 10. oxygen

Lesson 22, page 69: A. 1. irresponsible 2. abstain 3. interpose 4. malformed 5. abduct 6. irrational **B.** 1. retroactive 2. intersection 3. malfunction 4. retrospective **page 70: A.** 1. abstain 2. malformed 3. intersection 4. abduct 5. retrospective 6. interpose 7. irresponsible 8. malfunction 9. irrational 10. retroactive **B.** 1. cross 2. abstain 3. rocket 4. fight **page 71:** 1. a highway that goes among states

2. not regular 3. discontented person 4. not normal 5. lacking in respect 6. not present 7. mutual dependence 8. a virus that produces tumors using RNA instead of DNA 9. poor nutrition 10. a rocket that can reverse the motion of an aircraft or spacecraft

Lesson 23, page 72: A. 1. illiterate 2. hydroplane 3. commiserate 4. illegal 5. compile 6. monotone **B.** 1. bivalve 2. monosyllable 3. hydroelectric 4. biannual **page 73: A.** 1. compile 2. monosyllable 3. hydroelectric 4. biannual 5. bivalve 6. commiserate 7. illegal 8. monotone 9. hydroplane 10. illiterate **B.** 1. notes 2. bivalve 3. mouth 4. ill **page 74:** 1. monochrome 2. biweekly 3. monorail 4. compress 5. illegible 6. hydrometer 7. monolingual or bilingual 8. hydrofoil 9. commotion

Lesson 24, page 75: A. 1. denouncement, charge 2. relaxation, play 3. noble, courageous 4. disorderly, unruly 5. renowned, celebrated 6. juicy, fleshy 7. hopefulness, cheerfulness **B.** 1. dentist 2. journalism 3. perfectionist **page 76: A.** 1. recreation 2. dentist 3. turbulent 4. historic 5. optimism 6. journalism 7. succulent 8. perfectionist 9. heroic 10. accusation **B.** 1. air 2. recreation 3. optimism 4. succulent **page 77:** Answers will vary.